PREFACE

"If you run, you are a runner. It doesn't matter how fast or how far. It doesn't matter if today is your first day or if you've been running for twenty years. There is no test to pass, no license to earn, no membership card to get. You just run."

-John Bingham

INTRODUCTION: SAYING YES

So you want to run cross-country. It sounds easy, right? After all, it's just putting one foot in front of the other. How hard can it be?

> *"Running is real and relatively simple... but it ain't easy."* -Mark Will-Weber

Well, it's actually quite a bit more complicated than that. For beginners, running is easy ... for about eight seconds. Then you'll question what you've gotten yourself into. And you'll ask yourself that same question many, many times.

Committing to run almost every day for the next four years is no small commitment. There will be highs and lows. There will be days you'll feel like you can run forever, and days you'll barely make it out the front door. There will be tears of both happiness and despair.

You'll sweat more than you thought humanly possible. You'll probably trip over your own two feet, or a rock, or a root, or a curb, and likely leave some skin behind. You'll probably get injured at some point, and the injury might cause you to stop running for a while. Then, *not* running will drive you crazy because it's all you'll want to do.

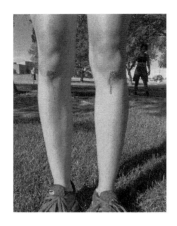

Running Tip #1: It will be unpleasant at first.

Your improvement in the first few months will be shocking to you. I've seen kids who could barely run across the gym suddenly running three to four miles with ease after just a month or two of training. The capability of the human body to adapt to the demands of running every day is extraordinary. The speed of your improvement will surprise you.

Joining your middle or high school's cross-country team is more than just a commitment to run every day. It's also a commitment to your new team, your teammates, your school, your coach, and, most importantly, yourself. The reasons for joining any sport are varied: perhaps you fancy yourself a good runner, or maybe you're using cross-country as a way to make friends. Maybe you have another reason entirely. Regardless, cross-country teams tend to be all-inclusive, no-cut, and supportive of teammates regardless of ability. Cross-country teams and teammates almost always reward hard work over talent. You'll always have the respect and adoration of your teammates as long as you work hard, display a commitment to the team, and don't complain. You'll be accepted whether you're the fastest or the slowest kid on the team.

Running Tip #2: It gets easier.

Nobody starts running and feels awesome on day one. The first couple of weeks will be painful and hard. Your thoughts will be focused on how much the last step hurt and how much the next step will hurt even more. Then, after about two to three weeks, running will suddenly get easier. You'll run a distance that seemed impossible two weeks earlier. You'll complete it and realize you weren't thinking of each and every dreadful step during that run. It will be a great moment, because from that point on, you can focus on all the other things your coach may want you to think about during the run, rather than the initial suffering.

> "A run begins the moment you forget you are running."
>
> -Adidas advertisement

The individuals you'll meet on your team will likely remain in your life for a long, long time. The bonds of friendship grow stronger through shared adversity, and there will be plenty of adversity! The rigors of daily training and racing will forge connections that will never be broken.

Your new team will, of course, have a coach—or multiple coaches, depending on the size of your school and your cross-country teams. Some schools have a coed coach for both boys and girls combined, and some schools have separate coaches for each gender. Your new coach may be a former Olympian or someone who's never run a step. Either person can make an awesome coach or an awful coach—a coach doesn't *have* to be a great runner to be a great coach. A coach who is or was a runner can be helpful, though. They can relate to you as an athlete. They'll understand how hard this sport is, and mentor you appropriately. If they're a runner, they'll just "get it."

At every level, from youth track to college, there are good coaches and there are not-so-good coaches, and a lot in between. If you're like most kids, you don't get to choose your middle or high school, and you get what you get for a coach. If you live in a larger city, you might be able to choose your school through an open-enrollment system. With open enrollment, you have an opportunity to choose the school whose team has the best reputation, or the best results, or the coach with the best reputation, or other criteria that matter to you.

Running Tip #3: Your 100 percent effort never changes. You just get a whole lot faster.

You'll learn a lot about yourself doing cross-country. You'll also learn just what your body can do—including how far you can push it before it says "no more." As you develop as a runner, the knowledge of how hard you can push yourself will become instinctual. The only change will be the speed you're running at. At first, a maximal effort might be a ten-minute mile, and three years later, that same level of effort will result in a five-minute mile. You'll produce the same maximal effort, but you'll be running a whole lot faster.

Now that you've said yes to joining a cross-country team, it's time to learn how to be successful at this sport.

"The miracle isn't that I finished. The miracle is that I had the courage to start." -John Bingham

1

EQUIPMENT

Running cross-country is no different than participating in any other middle or high school sport. You wouldn't show up to the first day of soccer practice without cleats, would you? Or go to tennis practice without a racquet? Cross-country requires equipment too.

Compared to many other sports, however, cross-country is fairly inexpensive. You could even show up in jeans and flip-flops, but I don't think you'd enjoy that running experience very much. Instead, let's make sure you have the equipment basics for cross-country before you show up for your first day of practice.

> "A pair of running shoes and a dream can take you anywhere." -RunTheEdge

FOOTWEAR:

Trainers

Traditional training shoes, or trainers, feature a soft midsole that acts as a cushion between your body and the ground. They've been the mainstay of the running community since the mid-1970s, and they comprise about 98 percent of all running shoes sold.

You'll spend the vast majority of your practice time in trainers, and most new cross-country runners will also race in them. Trainers are the most important piece of equipment you'll buy, so take your time, do your research, and buy a good pair. Here are a few things to keep in mind before you buy.

Drop

An important, yet often overlooked, aspect of a trainer is the "drop." The drop is the difference between the heel midsole thickness and the forefoot midsole thickness.

A great way to envision this concept is a flip-flop. The heel thickness and forefoot thickness are identical in a flip-flop, resulting in a heel-to-toe drop of zero. The opposite would be a high-heeled shoe, where the heel is considerably higher than the forefoot. A high heel has a really high drop.

Drop is measured in millimeters. Anything near or below zero is considered a "minimalist" shoe. A mid-level drop is anything between four and seven millimeters. Anything over eight millimeters is a pretty large drop. In the mid-1980s, high-drop trainers were all the rage, with drops of as much as fourteen millimeters.

So why is the drop important? Because a large drop encourages overstriding and a big heel strike on the ground: that's what all the extra heel cushioning was designed to help with. The problem is that a big heel strike is a result of poor running form, and it actually slows you down. We'll delve into proper running form in chapter 3.

Running Tip #4: Tie your shoes! And double-knot them!

Seriously: tie them as snugly as you can without losing sensation in your feet. Running shoes are designed to behave in a certain way while attached to you.

If your laces are loose, the shoes will behave differently (read: worse) than they should. Loose laces also increase your risk of injury.

Midsole Thickness

The thickness of the midsole can vary from shoe to shoe. Is a thicker midsole better? Maybe. There are some shoe companies, like Hoka One One, that offer very thick and cushiony midsoles. There are also many shoes available that have half the midsole thickness of a Hoka. Both the Hokas and the thinner-soled shoes are popular, and fine for trainers.

Minimalist Trainers

Minimalist training shoes have none of the soft, cushiony midsole material of traditional running shoes. The design of the shoe promotes a forefoot running style, and the theory behind it is that your heel shouldn't be making a big impact with the ground, so there's no need for all that cushioning.

The minimalist-shoe trend was popular from around 2005 to 2012, but it's mostly died away. The reason the general popularity of minimalist shoes declined was because in order to effectively run in minimalist shoes, you must have a very specific running form. Any other running form and you greatly increase the risk of injury. As a result, they've become harder to find in stores.

Only wear your trainers when you're running—they only have so much life in them. Don't use them up by wearing them around school.

Running Tip #5: Your running shoes are not your everyday shoes.

Durability

How long do traditional trainers last? That depends on the trainers (brand, style) and you (size, running form). On average, a pair of trainers will last around five hundred miles. A trainer that's seen too many miles is less resilient, and becomes less and less protective with each mile.

Eventually, you'll begin to feel "beat up" from running. That's usually a sign that it's time for some new shoes. This is why it's a really good idea to track the number of miles you've put on your shoes. Simply write down when you bought your new pair of trainers, track the mileage you put on them, and replace them before you get to that point of feeling beat up.

Shopping for Trainers

If there's a specialty running store (a store that only sells running gear) within an hour of your house, buy your shoes there. They have the expertise to guide you, they don't carry low-quality brands, and they'll usually let you try on multiple pairs and jog around the parking lot in them so you can determine the best-fitting shoe for you. Don't go to a giant sports retail store—those stores don't have knowledgeable staff, and they typically only carry lower-end trainers.

Remember, you're going to spend a lot of time in these trainers, and they'll be the only things between you and the ground for many, many miles. Sure, you can find a forty-dollar pair of knockoff trainers at a discount store, but they'll be trashed and worn out in about ninety miles. Spend a hundred dollars and get a pair of trainers that will last for five hundred miles.

Racing Flats

Racing flats are a bit like minimalist training shoes, but made with lighter materials and without some of the extra protective rubber found on the trainers. They'll have a drop of two to three millimeters.

Why are racing shoes different from training shoes? There are two big reasons. First, they're lighter, and lighter is faster. Running a 5K will equate to roughly four thousand to six thousand strides. Even just a tiny difference in shoe weight adds up over the course of that many strides. Your brain will notice the difference in weight, and you'll run faster. Second, their shape promotes a more responsive foot strike.

I know what you're thinking: "If racing shoes are so great, why don't they just make training shoes like racing shoes?" That's a really good question. The main reason is because racing flats wouldn't hold up to the rigors of everyday training, and neither would your body. They're great for races and hard workouts, but they simply aren't designed for everyday mileage.

This is why I recommend trainers with a mid-range drop of four to six millimeters. That isn't too far from the two-to-three-millimeter drop you'll experience in racing flats, which helps make the transition between flats and trainers less stressful on the body. If you train in trainers with a huge drop and then try and race in racing flats, it will cause a lot of micro-damage to your calves, and the day after the race you'll be crying about how your calves are trashed.

Racing flats have three basic designs: spikes (track spikes and cross-country spikes), spikeless flats, and road-racing flats. This is a cross-country book, so we won't talk about road-racing flats in detail, but sometimes you'll race on courses that have surfaces that render regular spikes, or even spikeless flats, less effective. This is where road-racing flats can offer an advantage.

Let's look at spikes and how they're used.

Spikes

The girl in the picture above is very proud of the multi-colored spikes she screwed in for the state championships. Spikes are racing flats, but with a series of screw-in spike receptacles beneath the forefoot of the shoe.

Cross-country spikes usually have a rubberized surface with four to six spike receptacles. The image at right shows this quite well. The excited girl in the previous picture was displaying track spikes, not cross-country spikes. Track spikes have a plastic plate under the forefoot.

Many cross-country courses use softer surfaces, like grass and dirt. Optimal traction, especially in wet or muddy conditions, can be hugely beneficial. One of the slipperiest surfaces to race on is a golf course in the early morning—all that dewy grass will cause your foot to slip backward with every stride, which will slow you down a lot. With spikes on, you won't slip, but your competitors will. Spikes give you the advantage.

SHORTS:

For shorts, anything will suffice, but some fabrics are better than others at dissipating moisture and reducing chafing. Finely woven nylon is lightweight, soft, and available in any running store. Running-specific shorts typically have a liner inside them similar to a bathing suit. Boys, take note: traditional running shorts are, well, short. They're short shorts.

HIGH SCHOOL

When you receive your uniform and see your shorts for the first time, many of you will recoil in horror. "No way am I wearing these!" you'll say. Just know that everyone, on every team, will be in the same short shorts.

Why are running shorts so short? Well, any extra fabric (like in basketball shorts that hit at or below the knee) just gets in the way. The entire sport of distance running is an exercise in efficiency, and bulky, oversized shorts are inefficient. However, true running shorts are designed to have fabric between your upper thighs in an effort to reduce chafing. Any runner who has ever chafed in this area knows what I'm talking about—it's horribly painful the following day. Basketball-style shorts aren't cut the same in the upper, inner thigh area, which leaves you vulnerable to the Chafing Monster. If you just can't don the short shorts, wear some compression shorts underneath them.

SHIRTS:

Anything goes in the shirt department. There are "tech" nylon shirts that work well, and many other "non-tech" nylon shirts that are awful. How can you tell the difference? Stick with shirts from reputable running-apparel companies, or made from a specific fabric that many companies use. Coolmax, for example, is a nylon weave that wicks moisture away from the body and releases it into the atmosphere, keeping you cooler when it's hot outside.

Generally speaking, cotton T-shirts work just fine most of the time. They can be troublesome on long runs of over ten miles, however. If the temperature is just right, they can be a disaster for guys because they can rub nipples raw. You don't want that!

True story

During my sophomore year of high school, our team got new uniforms. (Teams typically replace uniforms every four to six years or so.) We were psyched to have some new gear, and the singlets looked really nice. They were white with a broad blue band—bearing our school name—that went straight across the chest. There was a problem, though: whatever material they used to make that blue band across our chests was really, really abrasive. After a 5K race, that abrasive material would rub raw the nipples of every boy on the team. It became a pre-race ritual to place Band-Aids over our nipples for protection. Fun times!

RACE WEAR:

Race uniforms typically consist of a shorts and singlet combo. A singlet is sleeveless jersey-type top similar to a tank top. The governing body for high school sports, the National Federation of State High School Associations (NFHS) has a lot of rules regarding what appropriate clothing is and isn't. They've relaxed some of the rules about jewelry, and most recently about team uniforms having to be identical.

There are still many other rules regarding hats, gloves, socks, arm sleeves, sunglasses, and running barefoot, so it's helpful to know them all before you race. Your state organizing body may also have rules specific to your state. Your coach should be aware of these rules and make them clear early in the season—you definitely don't want to be disqualified from a race because of a rule you didn't know about.

WINTER WEAR:

Cold weather means that shorts and a T-shirt are not going to be adequate. Sweatpants or tights with a sweatshirt or running jacket should be fine under most conditions, and a hat, headband, and gloves or mittens are crucial if it's really cold. One rule of thumb is to add fifteen degrees to the outside temperature: that's what it will feel like while running.

> **Running Tip #6: When it's cold and windy, always run *into* the wind (headwind) first, and *with* the wind (tailwind) on the way home.**

If you run the first half of your run with the wind behind you, it will feel much warmer, and you'll likely work up a nice sweat underneath all your layers of clothing. But when you turn around into the headwind, it will suddenly feel much, much colder, and now that you're wet from sweating, it will be a miserable—and possibly dangerous—run back.

Always wear more than you think necessary—you can always take a layer off and tie it around your waist. Over the years, I've accumulated many hats, headbands, gloves, and mittens. Each is good for a certain temperature range. I have mittens that I only wear when it's below twenty degrees. I have other gloves that I wear at thirty-five degrees. The same goes for hats and headbands, running tights, shirts, and jackets. Accumulate many and find the temperature zone where each is most effective. And take special precaution when it's windy! Remember to run into the wind first and then with the wind on the way back.

True story

In high school, I had a twelve-miler planned. It was windy, forty degrees, and lightly raining. As I ran the first six miles with the wind behind me, I felt warm enough in my long-sleeve cotton T-shirt, even though it was getting a little wet. Then I turned around. Now I was in a wet cotton T-shirt, running into a twenty-mile-per-hour headwind, and the temperature had dropped to thirty-five degrees. In three miles I

> *had gotten so cold and hypothermic that I decided to stop and hitchhike the last three miles home. When I arrived home, my hands were so cold that I couldn't even grip the doorknob strongly enough to get the door open. Luckily, someone was home to let me in.*

SUMMER WEAR:

Your body stays cool in two ways. First is through what's called radiation: your skin surface gets hotter then the air temperature, so heat radiates from your body into the atmosphere. For radiation to work well, you need a lot of exposed skin, while of course remaining decent. The other way the body cools itself is through the evaporation of sweat, also called evaporative cooling. As a liquid becomes a gas, it cools. As sweat evaporates from your skin surface, it cools your skin surface.

Each person is unique, and their body will utilize their own personal combination of radiation and evaporative cooling to cool down. We've all seen that kid who sweats literally gallons of water on a simple, short run, while another kid barely sweats at all. We're all different—it doesn't mean one person is working harder than the other.

In the summer, be wary of cotton. Cotton tends to hold the moisture against the body, increasing body temperature. It's also helpful to remember that, from a clothing perspective, the color white reflects the sun. White shirts help reflect the sun's rays; a white cap helps keep the head cool for the same reason. Special fabrics that wick moisture away from the body are helpful as well.

One trick for running in hot weather is to fill a disposable water bottle with water and freeze it solid. Run with the bottle in the palms of your hands: your hands and feet are great for dissipating heat through direct radiation. Your body will transfer heat to the frozen bottle right through the palms of your hands. It will keep your core body temperature down and you'll have a better run. Plus, you can drink it as it melts.

In the summertime, it's common to run shirtless, or in just a sports bra for girls. Your school may or may not allow this. Remember, when you're out there on the roads and trails around your community, you're representing your team, and your school. What's appropriate for young boys and girls to wear while running countless miles is at the discretion of your school's athletic department and your coach. When I was coaching, I allowed boys to be shirtless and girls to be in sports bras while off campus. Once they were back on campus or in the school (in the gym or weight room, for example), it was shirts on at all times.

2
─────────────────────────

HOW YOUR BODY WORKS

MUSCLES:

Before we delve into muscles and how they work, I am going to provide you a synopsis of what this chapter hopes to accomplish. Understanding how your body works, and your muscles in particular, is extremely important. This chapter is a bit detailed, however the information within it will help you to improve as a runner. It will describe the difference between concentric and eccentric muscle contractions and when you engage each. It will also identify and describe each of the six main muscle groups in your lower body, and how they apply to your running body.

Your muscles are what move your body in various directions. For the purposes of this book, they move you forward while running. How do they do that, exactly?

Well, each muscle is attached to a bone at one end, and then it crosses a joint (where two bones meet) and attaches to another bone on the other side of that joint. When the muscle contracts and gets shorter (a concentric contraction), it causes the joint to bend in a certain direction, depending on the force that the muscle places on it.

Let's test this. If you're currently sitting down, lift your knee off the chair and concentrically contract (shorten) your quadriceps (thigh). Notice your lower leg rise as your knee joint bends and your foot moves upward and away from you. This is a simplified example, of course, but it's an easy way to start to understand how your muscles work.

Every muscle in your body has a specific function; it has one job to do. In your arm, for example, your bicep concentrically contracts and your forearm moves upward toward your shoulder into a basic curl. When your bicep produces a force, your forearm can either move upward—concentric contraction—or it can resist a downward force — eccentric contraction. This is called an eccentric contraction because the muscle is lengthening while contracting.

To test out an eccentric contraction, place your hand up by your shoulder and have a friend try to force your hand downward. It's still your bicep that's producing force, but now it's resisting the downward pressure. The bicep is elongating as your friend forces your hand downward, so it's an eccentric contraction.

When we get to the next chapter, on running form, it will

be really helpful to understand what each muscle in your legs does while running, and how they all work together in harmony. Knowing how the body is supposed to move will help you use all of your muscles in an efficient and effective way, and you'll run faster because of it.

Here are some examples of what each of the main leg muscle groups are supposed to do.

Glutes

Your butt muscles: gluteus maximus, medius, and minimus.

The glutes have one purpose: to take your femur (thigh), and throw it backward. Now, you might be thinking, "But when I run, my thigh doesn't go backward." Actually, it does, relative to the rest of your body. Have you ever tried to run on ice? What happens? Your thigh goes flying backward because your foot isn't tethered to the ground, and you move absolutely nowhere. When your foot has traction on the ground, your thigh can't go backward, so your body must go forward. That's how you move forward. Believe it or not, your glutes are 90 percent responsible for moving you forward.

Quadriceps

The muscles in the front of each thigh: vastus lateralis, vastus medialis, rectus femoris, vastus intermedius

The purpose of the quadriceps, commonly called the quads, is to move the lower leg forward. When you're running, your quads act mostly in an eccentric manner. When your foot hits the ground, your knee bends a little and your quads resist your knee bending all the way so you don't crash to the ground in a heap. In other sports (soccer, football, basketball), the quads are used mostly as brakes, to slow you down.

Quads are important for running, but they contribute very little to forward movement. They're used mostly for stabilization and balance when landing after each stride. Your quads are also what you use to run backward!

Hamstrings

The muscles in the back of each thigh: biceps femoris, semitendinosus, and semimembranosus

There are two main functions of the hamstrings: the first is to move the lower leg backward (concentric contraction) or prevent your lower leg from moving forward (eccentric contraction). The second is to flex the hip joint backward.

When we think about how the hamstrings function in relation to other muscles, again, they serve two functions. First, they assist the glutes in moving the body forward by flexing the hip joint backward. Second, they act on the lower leg in the exact opposite direction of the quads.

To help visualize this, stand up and do a quick butt kick

with each leg. Your hamstrings are what move your foot up behind you during this exercise—this is a classic concentric contraction for the hamstrings.

During running, your hamstrings act in both a concentric and an eccentric manner: concentrically with reaction to the hip joint, and eccentrically with relation to the knee joint. Their main concentric task is to assist the glutes in moving the thigh backward. Their main eccentric task is to hold your knee in a stable position while slowly and slightly elongating. They do this so your glutes can do their work and throw the thigh backward. Think about it: if your hamstrings didn't work for some reason and you used your glutes to send your thigh backward, your knee would immediately snap backward and lock straight. That would look pretty funny out on the racecourse.

Calves

The backs of your lower legs: gastrocnemius and soleus are the main two

The gastrocnemius is the bigger, meatier, upper part of the calf. The soleus is below and underneath the gastrocnemius. The soleus connects to the Achilles tendon at the back of your heel.

Both of these muscles produce force that points the foot downward (plantar flexion). When you're running and your foot is touching the ground, you use your soleus (mostly) to flex that foot downward. Your foot can't go downward because the ground is in the way, however, so your body goes upward. This is mostly what provides the bounce to your running stride. If you happen to be leaning forward while running, the soleus can also provide a small amount of forward movement.

The gastrocnemius, on the other hand, is mostly a walking muscle. It fully engages when the knee is nearly straight, so only towards the very end of a running stride. The more the knee bends, the less the gastrocnemius is utilized, and the more the soleus is utilized. When you're running, you're mostly using your soleus.

To illustrate this, sit with your butt on the edge of a chair. Invite a friend to sit on your knees. Your soleus muscles are strong enough to do calf raises with your friend sitting on your knees. While doing these calf raises, feel your meaty gastrocnemius muscles. Notice that they're soft and not flexed at all. This is because they're not being used for this exercise, since your knees are bent at a ninety-degree angle.

Knowing which calf muscles work, and when, is important in the weight room. When doing calf raises with weights, always keep your knees a little bit bent. This will utilize the soleus more while lifting, and that's the muscle you want to develop more. I know the bigger one looks cooler, but it's the soleus that'll make you run faster.

Dorsiflexors

The front of your lower legs: tibialis anterior, peroneus longus, and peroneus brevis

These three muscles work together to pull the foot upward (dorsiflexion). They do the opposite of the calves. There isn't a lot of this motion in a human running gait, so these muscles are smaller. They're really important when talking about shin splints, however. We'll get to that in chapter 8.

Hip flexors

The front of your hips and pelvis: rectus femoris, iliacus, and others

The purpose of the hip flexors is to bring the thigh forward. This means they do the opposite of the glutes, which move the thigh backward. From a running standpoint, moving the thigh backward is far more important. That said, once your foot leaves the ground, that thigh must move forward so it can land underneath you again. This movement is the hip flexors at work. The rectus femoris is the main hip flexor when running.

So there you have it: these are the six main muscle groups in your legs. Notice we discussed how to move your thigh forward and backward, how to move your lower leg forward and backward, and how to move your foot up and down. These are most of the movement directions that apply to distance runners: you don't have to concern yourself very much with the muscles that help you move from side to side. (Tennis and soccer players, on the other hand, care a lot about these muscles.)

Also notice that all the muscles that move you forward are located behind you—glutes, hamstrings, calves—and all the muscles that slow you down are located in front of you—quads, hip flexors, and dorsiflexors. Neat, huh?

FUEL:

Your body utilizes two main fuel types while running: fat and carbohydrates (sugar). Each breaks down into something called adenosine triphosphate (ATP). Even as a high school kid, you pretty much know what these two fuel sources are, and what foods they're found in. We'll talk more about food in chapter 7, but for now, we're mostly interested in how your body utilizes these two fuel sources.

In general, you burn mostly fat when you aren't exerting yourself very much, like right now as you read this book. But if you were to put this book down and go run a fast mile on the track, your muscle's fuel source will be mostly carbohydrates. And if that mile turns into a 5K, you'll use a mix of fat and carbohydrates. As you go from a state of low activity to a state of intense activity, the fuel source transitions from fat to carbohydrates.

Why is this? Well, even though fats provide more energy per gram than carbohydrates, they produce that energy much slower. So, even though a gram of carbohydrates produces roughly 60 percent less energy than a gram of fat, carbohydrates produce it much, much faster. Therefore, when you're running a 5K, you can't run very fast on only fat as a fuel. Your body will need to burn carbohydrates too.

There's no speed at which you switch from one fuel source to the other, and at the speeds we're talking about in middle or high school cross-country, it will always be a mixture of both. The exception is in shorter track events, like a four-hundred-meter dash, where fat isn't really used at all. You don't sprint a 5K, however, so your body will utilize a mixture of both.

LUNGS, HEART, AND BLOOD:

Your lungs, heart, and blood are responsible for delivering oxygen from the air we breathe to the muscle cells that need it to burn fuel (fat and carbohydrates). Just like a campfire where you need fuel (wood) and oxygen, your body uses the same ingredients to create energy. Your blood is also the main way your body moves nutrients around (and a host of other things, like enzymes). For the purposes of this book, we'll focus mostly on the oxygen-delivery system.

When you run, your heart pumps blood throughout your body. That blood goes through your lungs, where it picks up oxygen from the air that's in your lungs. That oxygen-rich blood is then sent all over the body to the cells that need it. When you're running, your muscles need massive amounts of oxygen—this is why your heart rate increases. The point of a high heart rate is to move oxygen from the lungs and out to the muscles as quickly as possible in order to deliver as much oxygen as it can, as quickly as it can.

As you develop as a runner, your body will get better and better at delivering oxygen to your muscles. Your heart will get bigger and stronger. You'll make more blood, and the percentage of your blood that moves oxygen (red blood cells) will increase. Your arteries and veins will increase in size and stretchiness in order to accommodate the extra blood being pumped around at high speeds. You'll develop a lot more capillaries (tiny arteries in your muscles), to deliver even more oxygen to the cells that want it. In short, your body becomes an oxygen-moving machine.

THE STRETCH RELFEX:

Each muscle has millions of sensors that your brain monitors constantly. These sensors measure many things, including temperature, acidity, enzymatic activity, and the ones we really care about: muscle length. Yes, your brain monitors how long each muscle is at all times! It wants the length of your muscles to remain within a certain range because it knows that if your muscles get stretched too far, there is a risk of injury.

If your brain senses that a muscle, any muscle, is

stretching too far, too quickly, it will react to save the muscle from tearing by actually contracting the muscle. This is the stretch reflex, and it exists in all skeletal muscles in the human body.

The muscle can stretch farther than your brain leads you to think, but with increased risk (like the muscle actually tearing). Your brain monitors this and makes the stretch feel painful before you do some real damage.

Here's an example. When you're sitting upright and you get drowsy, say in class (or, for me as a kid, during church), your head will start to fall forward. Your head is fairly heavy, and as it falls forward, it accelerates and falls fairly quickly. Your brain registers this and recognizes that the muscles in the back of your neck are stretching too far, too fast. Your brain reacts by contracting the muscles in the back of the neck and jerking your head upward, usually startling you awake. This was really embarrassing in church!

The same thing happens in your Achilles tendon. When your foot hits the ground, regardless of whether it's a heel strike, mid-foot strike, or forefoot strike, your Achilles tendon stretches very quickly. Your brain perceives this and employs the stretch reflex by contracting the Achilles and the attached soleus muscle. This makes you run faster! The better you can optimize this phenomenon, the faster you'll run.

Another important stretch reflex occurs in a muscle called the rectus femoris. This muscle starts just below the boney protrusion in front of your hipbone, and goes straight down toward your kneecap. When you're running and your thigh moves backward very quickly (because your glutes are super strong), your brain says the muscle is stretching too far and too fast, and it contracts the muscle, which moves your thigh forward. You force your thigh backward, your brain automatically brings it forward again, and then you can repeat the process all over again. The human body is a pretty remarkable instrument.

NEWTON'S THIRD LAW:

"For every action, there is an equal and opposite reaction."

If you punch a wall, you're applying force to that wall, right? Well, the wall is also applying that same force to your fist—that's how you break your hand. This happens in running, too: with every step you take, you hit the ground with a force of up to three times your body weight. And according to Mr. Newton's third law, when you hit the ground with all that force, the ground also hits *you* with all that force.

There are two reasons why this is important to distance runners. First is because that's a lot of force for your body to absorb stride after stride. Your body does a great job of dissipating the force through your body, but it takes time to absorb and then dissipate all that force—typically about a quarter of a second.

This leads to the second reason this is important: the

forces that the ground delivers to you start in your feet, and as it's absorbed, not all of that force is dissipated. Some of it is stored, temporarily, as energy, in your Achilles tendon.

How is this possible? Well, with each step, your body has the ability to temporarily store some of the force it receives from the impact with the ground. This energy stored in your Achilles tendon is available for use, *if* you can contract your Achilles tendon quickly enough (the stretch reflex helps here). This makes you run faster. We'll talk more about how to better utilize this free energy in the next chapter.

3

RUNNING FORM

> "God determines how fast you're going to run; I can only help with the mechanics." -Bill Bowerman

Imagine two runners. They're each equally fit, and their bodies have the same ability to move oxygen. The first runner runs like Quasimodo from *The Hunchback of Notre Dame*—his knees buckle inward, his feet flare out and land too far apart. His torso seems to go from side to side like he's zigzagging down the road. He bends over too much, which causes his butt to stick out behind him. His head goes forward and back with every stride, which makes him look like a pigeon. His arms flail about like he just got pushed into the deep end of a pool but doesn't know how to swim.

The second runner, in contrast, looks smooth. His legs and feet are tracking straight, his arms aren't all over the place, his torso position is perfect, and his head is still.

Which of these two runners will win the race every time? You guessed it: the second one. If they both have the same ultimate potential on race day, then the one who best utilizes that potential wins. While the first runner uses a ton of energy on wasted movements, the second runner wastes no energy. Every ounce of the second runner's energy is dedicated to moving forward.

THE TWO THEORIES OF RUNNING:

There are two main theories on how running happens. The first is that running is a controlled fall. The second is that running is a series of successive hops. Let's unpack each one of these a little bit.

When I think of a controlled fall, I like to think of a unicycle. When a unicyclist wants to move forward, they can't just start pedaling or they'll fall over backward. They must lean forward and pedal at the same time in order to be successful, and, more importantly, stay upright. By leaning forward, gravity pulls the unicyclist downward, just a little bit and they must pedal with enough force to resist that forward fall. The more they lean over, the faster they have to pedal, or else what? They'll fall forward onto their face.

According to the controlled-fall theory of how running

happens, the same is true. As you lean forward, you have to move one of your legs forward and underneath you in order to arrest your "fall." Then, you must move the other leg forward, and so on and so on. The more you lean forward, the faster you have to move your legs, just to stay upright. This is gravity at work, trying to pull you down—and you're letting it, to a point. Proponents of this theory say that this running style is more efficient because you're only using your leg muscles to *prevent you from falling*, not push you forward, and preventing you from falling requires much less energy.

The successive-hops theory is very different. When I think of this theory, I like to think of an ostrich. Ostriches are extremely powerful birds that run on two legs, like humans. An ostrich generates a massive amount of forward force off of one leg, sails through the air, and then lands on the other leg. Then it repeats the process. It sounds very simple, and it is.

So which running theory is right? Well, there are two different camps on this. I believe that both are right. How can both be right? Well, the controlled fall works, but only up to a certain speed. Think back to that unicyclist. Sure, if he leans forward a little bit, he can pedal fast enough to move forward and stay upright. If he leans too far forward, though, he simply can't pedal fast enough, and he'll fall forward. There's a limit to how fast the unicyclist can go.

The same holds true for running. You can only lean over so far, because your legs can only go so fast to get underneath you before you tumble forward. There comes a speed at which your leg speed is the limiting factor with the controlled fall, and to go any faster, you have to start using your legs to propel you forward (successive hops, like the ostrich).

Depending on your height and body dimensions, the maximum speed you can run through a controlled fall is around an eleven-minute mile. This is why the controlled fall method is popular with ultra-marathoners. When running one hundred miles, efficiency, not speed, is paramount.

But you aren't an ultra-marathoner. You're a middle or a high school 5K runner, or a miler on the track. Eleven-minute miles won't win you a 5K, let alone a mile on the track. So, you'll need to utilize the successive-hops theory to run fast. There's a reason why the ostrich is the third-fastest animal on the planet!

Good running form will, very simply, help you run faster and stay injury-free. And staying injury-free is a big part of distance running—it's hard to improve as a runner if you're constantly injured.

How do you know if you have good running form or not? One of the best ways is to have someone shoot some video of you running. Have them get angles from the front and the side—each of these angles will reveal many things.

Now let's examine the components of running form: your torso, your legs, and your arms.

COMPONENTS OF RUNNING FORM:

Your Torso

For our purposes, your torso is everything above your legs, not including your arms. (Yes, this means your head too!)

A runner should lean forward slightly, by about 2 or 3 percent. Remember, you want to utilize gravity as part of that controlled fall. How do you measure 2 to 3 percent? You have to get a giant protractor. Just kidding. It's a bit easier than that. When you're standing still, lean forward until your eyes are right over your toes. Assuming you don't have enormous, or tiny, feet, this is about 2 to 3 percent.

When running, as your foot is starting to lift off the ground, you should be able to draw a straight line from your ankle, to your hip, to your shoulder. If you bend at the waist, you won't have a straight line. So, be sure to bend from the ankles.

Additionally, watch out for any side-to-side bobbing of your torso. Some kids look like they're in a boxing match with how violently they're moving from side to side as they run. That's simply wasted motion.

Your Legs and Feet

You probably guessed that your legs and feet are pretty important components of your running form. You'd be right!

HIGH SCHOOL

First things first: make sure your legs are only moving forward and backward. Minimize any sideways movement. Your knees shouldn't crash inward on each stride, and your foot shouldn't flare out as it returns underneath you.

True story

We had a girl on our team whose feet flared outward so badly that her team nickname was "Mashed Potatoes," after the dance of the same name. (You flail your feet out to the sides in this dance.)

Another big issue is where your feet should land on every stride. Once your foot leaves the ground after you've pushed off, it moves forward and then it has to land again, somewhere. The graphic above is pretty simple, but it accurately displays where you want your foot to land. The "bad" side represents overstriding.

When I think of overstriding, I picture walking on stilts, which is another example of a controlled fall. As the stilt walker leans forward, she must move one stilt forward to a spot right underneath herself, and then repeat the process. But what happens if she suddenly sticks one stilt way out in front of her? Well, the stilt she stuck way out there will act as a brake, and stop her dead in her tracks.

This is exactly what happens when you throw your leg too far forward while running. Look at that "bad" image again. That forward leg acts as a brake. With each step, the poor runner slows down just a little bit, and then has to use extra energy to reaccelerate. And they have to do this on every single stride, for miles. This is inefficient and wasteful.

Now look at the "good" image. Her foot lands barely in front of her center of gravity. Because it's immediately underneath her (not out in front of her), it doesn't act as a brake. Instead, the forward leg is ready to move forward the instant it touches down. Also, notice that her eyes are above her toes.

Most beginning runners will overstride. Your coach should be aware of this and give you cues to help avoid it. Runners that overstride incur higher injury rates, according to a 2014 study by Schubert, Kempf, & Heiderscheit.

So, what should your feet do when you run? For decades, there have been discussions around whether your heel, forefoot, or mid-foot should strike the ground first. If your torso and legs are doing what they are supposed to do, then your feet should naturally contact the ground in a beneficial way. Anywhere from a very slight heel strike to a very slight forefoot strike has been proven to be the sweet spot for an effective landing. So, do what's most comfortable for you. We'll talk about the perils of severe heel and forefoot strikes in the "how they all work together" section of this chapter.

Your Arms

Your arms are more important than you think. Most of the time during training, your arms are pretty much just along for the ride, sort of like a T. rex's. But as you go faster, like in races and faster workouts, your arms become more important.

From a running-form perspective, the same principles of directional motion that applied to the legs also apply to the arms. You want your arms moving mostly forward and backward. Keep your elbows in—don't look like a chicken with its wings out when you're running.

A common question is what angle should your elbows be at? That is, should your hands be lower (by your hips) or up higher (by your chest)? There are world-class distance runners who hold their hands a little low, and there are world-class distance runners who hold them a little high. To be safe, try the middle somewhere. Again, do what's most comfortable for you.

Regardless of how high or low you hold your hands, however, there is one massive running-form problem that plagues many runners—even elite ones. The problem is that they don't swing their arms at all. Instead, they twist their torso and shoulders to move one shoulder forward and the opposing shoulder backward, which presents the *illusion* of swinging arms.

The range of motion for your arms will vary based on how fast you're going. When you're out for an easy run, your arms will only swing a little. When you're running fast, like during strides or faster interval training, they'll experience a much larger range of motion. That huge range of motion, when running fast, will really highlight any form issues with your arms. During this faster running, many coaches preach "cheek to cheek," meaning your hands should move from your cheek (face) to your cheek (butt). This is the maximum range of motion you want when running fast.

Running Tip #7: Twisting your torso isn't swinging your arms.

To actually swing your arms, they must pivot at the shoulder. This means that all the forward and backward movement originates at the shoulder. You should have a little shoulder sway to counterbalance all the twisting force of your hips and lower body, but it shouldn't masquerade as arm swinging.

HOW THEY ALL WORK TOGETHER:

As a middle or high school student, you may not be able to articulate what good running form is, but you'll likely know it when you see it. Some runners make running look easy—they just float along effortlessly. That's in large part because they have efficient running form.

Remember the stretch reflex and Newton's third law: if you're a massive overstrider, you'll likely be a huge heel-striker. You'll receive a large impact force from the ground, due to Newton's third law. Because you've put your foot down way out in front of your center of gravity, your foot will be on the ground (also called ground contact time) for so long, that those forces being stored in your Achilles tendon will, in part, dissipate before you get a chance to use them. Remember, those forces are free energy that you don't have to produce, so losing any portion of that energy, because you're overstriding, is another inefficiency. Not taking advantage of free energy is never a good option. Overstriding also reduces the effect of the stretch reflex in your Achilles tendon: because of the dynamics of landing heel-first with your leg way out in front of you, the stretch of the Achilles is slower and shorter, thus less effective in creating a strong stretch reflex in your lower leg. This is also inefficient.

If you're a huge forefoot striker (so much so that your heel never touches the ground), then your foot, ankle, and lower leg absorb all the free energy that comes from the impact with the ground. By dampening that impact with an over-exaggerated forefoot strike, you lose a lot of those impact forces. Why would you not want to use that free energy?

To summarize good running form, run tall and in a straight line. Keep all your body parts moving forward and backward, not sideways. And, most importantly, don't overstride.

4

TRAINING

Improving as a runner involves a little more than just running—if you simply run three miles every day at nine minutes per mile, you'll be perfectly trained to run exactly three miles at nine minutes per mile. No faster. No longer.

To get faster, you'll need to run a variety of different distances at a variety of different speeds. Many of the basic workouts that most middle or high school kids will undertake are outlined later in this chapter.

The recent book *Peak Performance*, by Brad Stulberg and Steve Magness, boils growth down to a formula. This is the formula you'll want to remember for improving as a distance runner:

$$Stress + Rest = Growth$$

Stress, in this instance, is running. And yes, rest is as important as the workouts themselves. This is because when you're running, you're actually breaking your body down. It's while you rest, and sleep, that your body repairs all the damage done while running. This is true of all sports: when you repair the damage, you build yourself up just a little bit stronger than you were the day before. That's how you get better: just run every day, and every night you get a little fitter than you were.

This premise is why the generally accepted key to running success is consistency. Run every day (or six out of seven if your team mandates a day off every week). Provide your body with that stress stimulus every day, and you get a little stronger every night. It's amazing to watch kids join cross-country never having done a sport in their lives, and improve each and every day. Some can't even run across the gym on the first day of practice. But, they stick with it—they run every day, they get stronger every day, and after four years, some end up getting scholarships to run in college. This happens over and over. You don't have to be great on day one. With commitment, you'll be great eventually.

TRAINING BASICS:

Distance and Speed

Any runner hoping to run any race has to be able to do two things. First, they have to be able to run the distance. Second, they have to be able to run, to physically move their body, at the speed they want to run that race in.

For example, if your race is a mile, then, at a minimum, you must be able to run one mile. The hard part about the mile isn't running a mile, however—it's how fast you'll need to run it to be competitive. A miler's training will mainly consist of trying to make them faster. If, however, your race is a marathon, being able to run 26.2 miles becomes the driving factor that will dictate your training, not how fast you can sprint 100 meters.

Even if you're a newbie to cross-country, running five kilometers (without walking), will soon be easy enough. And, during faster and shorter workouts, you'll see that you can run much faster than your current 5K race pace. Once you can cover the distance and you can run pretty fast (for shorter distances), the trick becomes, how do you bring those two pieces together? How do you run the 5K distance faster? Your coach will have a training plan to help you to do just that. Some coaches share their training plan with the team, and some don't. Some will reveal it one week at a time. If you're new to cross-country, you won't really care about how all the various workouts fit together like a jigsaw puzzle. Trust that your coach is competent and has a well-designed plan to develop you into a great runner.

Outlined below are some basic training principles you should be aware of, as well as the different types of workouts you'll likely undertake as a middle or high school cross-country runner.

Hard/Easy Days

The single most important concept in distance running is that of alternating hard days with easy days. One way to improve as a runner is to push beyond your comfort zone. This can't be done every day. The human body can't handle that level of stress day after day. Alternating hard days with easy days allows the body to recover from the previous hard effort and to be prepared for the next one. This is called super-compensation.

Hard/Easy Weeks and Seasons

Just like alternating hard and easy days, many high school and college teams will also alternate hard and easy weeks. Mileage and intensity will increase for a "hard" week, and then ease off for an "easy" week, and so on. At my school, we would set our meet schedule up in a way that it had challenging meets every other week. By doing this, we could align our hard/easy training weeks with the hard/easy races, which allowed us to be fresher and more race-ready for the important competitions.

Another bigger picture view of hard/easy is the cross-country and track seasons themselves. They're in the fall and spring, respectively. This allows an opportunity to ease off somewhat during the off seasons and create hard/easy seasons.

Running Tip #8: Warming up and cooling down are a lot more important than you think.

Warming up prior to a hard workout or race is crucial for two reasons. First, it helps prepare your body for the rigors of what is to come. Secondly, it can help prevent injury. Your coach and your team will have a typical warm-up routine—it will likely include jogging followed by dynamic drills. Cooling down after a race or workout is equally important. Racing is very stressful on your body, and when you cool down post-race, you gently process all the byproducts of racing out of your muscles and into your liver, where they can be dealt with. Cooling down always makes you feel better the following day. A typical high school cool down usually consists of ten to fifteen minutes of light jogging and maybe some dynamic or static stretching.

Volume (Mileage)

Most middle or high school newbies nearly pass out when they hear the mileage that varsity kids run every day. With time, and commitment, your mileage will increase naturally. As you progress through your running career, you'll become stronger. And as you become stronger, your capacity to handle higher volume (distance) will increase.

Sometimes freshmen feel like they're getting shortchanged because coaches will recommend a lower overall volume, but it's a protective measure: no runner runs their best if they're injured. It's unwise for a freshman to run ten miles per day—no matter how much they want to—if they want to survive the season uninjured. The other side of that coin is some freshmen see the mileage that some upperclassmen are running and can't fathom running that much. Don't worry: with age and experience, it is indeed possible.

There are four basic factors that your coach will look at to determine how many miles you should be running every week: your "running" age, your "other sport" age, your durability, and your ability.

1. Your "running" age: Your running age is how many years you've been running. Let's say that I have two freshmen show up on day one of practice: one has never run a day in her life, and the other has been running middle school cross-country for three years.

A good coach won't lump these two runners together just because they're both freshman. Chronological age means very little. One has a running age of three, and the other has a running age of zero. They should be treated differently.

The same goes for the senior who finally decides to give cross-country a try. Just because he's a senior doesn't mean he can, or should, run what the other, experienced, seniors are running.

2. Your "other sport" age: In this example, think of a kid who's been playing soccer for eight years wants to join cross-country. This kid will have a completely different level of fitness than the kid who has never participated in a sport. The soccer kid will be able to handle a little more mileage right out of the gate.

3. Your durability: Another factor determining just how much mileage any given runner can handle is based on their durability. Simply put, some individuals are more durable to the rigors of distance running than others. Over the years I've coached kids that thrived on a running diet of higher mileage with no problems, and others that seemed to develop numerous small injuries off of very low mileage. These "durable" runners will often be allowed to run more mileage. The lower mileage kids supplemented their mileage with cross training, like swimming, biking, or elliptical workouts.

4. Your ability: How fast a kid is should never drive the amount of mileage they run. Younger and newer runners should always be on a diet of lower mileage at first, building that volume as they develop throughout middle and high school.

Even if a new freshman can run a race fast due to extraordinary natural ability, this doesn't mean they should go straight into running varsity-level mileage. This is a big mistake. All runners, at every ability level, should develop slowly, with the long-term-improvement view in mind.

Intensity (Speed)

There are two sayings in the running community that seem to be at odds with each other. The first is "train slow to run fast"; the other is "speed kills—it kills someone who doesn't have any."

So do you need speed-work, or can you be successful on a diet of slow mileage? The answer is, you need both—but mostly slow mileage. A 2011 study by E. Enoksen, showed that world-class runners ran 75 to 80 percent of their miles at paces slower than their race pace.

These elite runners recognize that mileage comprises the bulk of their miles, but that speedwork is necessary for success. Your team will introduce faster running to you in a variety of workouts, and with strides, to teach your body how to move faster.

Workouts

Should you run more or less? Faster or slower? There are numerous ways to vary distance, pace, and rest in order to elicit certain stresses on the body, which will produce improvements in the desired areas.

For high school runners, you're mostly looking to properly execute the basic workouts outlined below. Workouts get more complex and precise in college and beyond.

Racing: The obvious workout. Races are the ultimate "hard" day.

Easy, or recovery, runs: Easy runs are generally shorter and at a conversational pace. A good guideline for conversational pace is roughly 5K race pace plus two to three minutes per mile. By increasing blood flow into your muscles, easy runs increase muscle recovery from a previous hard day's effort. They also keep the muscles limber and prepare them for the next day's hard effort.

Long runs: A long run will be done about once a week, and will comprise roughly 20 percent of a runner's weekly mileage. Long runs are usually done at a conversational pace. Long runs obviously increase a runner's stamina, but they also improve a number of other things. They will certainly make you mentally stronger.

Threshold (tempo) workouts: Described as "comfortably hard," threshold runs are a hard workout. There are a few differing types of threshold workouts. The most popular, yet the most challenging to execute, is a single "threshold run," also called a tempo run. It's traditionally a twenty- to twenty-five-minute run at a lactate threshold (LT) pace, which is anywhere from fifteen to forty-five seconds per mile slower than a 5K race pace.

Another way to stimulate the LT is by running a series of repetitions at, or even slightly faster than, LT pace, with very short rest in between. These LT repetitions seem very easy at first but become increasingly difficult as the workout progresses, due to the short recovery time.

VO$_2$ max workouts: These are your classic interval workouts—repeats of anything from four hundred meters to two miles. The pace is 5K race pace, and recovery between the repetitions is long.

Running economy (RE) workouts: These are short, fast repetitions. The pace is around a 600M to 800M race pace. The recovery interval in between reps is long. The focus of these reps is form, form, and yes, say it again with me, form.

Most runners' form improves the faster they run, so RE workouts deliver a great bang for the buck. These workouts aren't particularly difficult, and they yield great results through improved efficiency. As an added bonus, RE workouts also stimulate the acid tolerance system (see below).

Acid tolerance workouts: Acid tolerance workouts are done primarily during track, as they have limited value during cross-country. The purpose is to prepare the athlete, both physically and mentally, for the final half of an 800M or 1600M race. The workouts are designed to produce acid early and follow it with race-pace work, thus introducing fast running in an acidic environment.

An example acid tolerance workout is three hundred meters at 99 percent, fifteen seconds' rest, and then eight hundred meters at mile-race pace.

These workouts mimic race scenarios in some ways, and most runners say they're the hardest workout they ever do.

Fartlek runs: Swedish for "speed play," fartlek is just that. A typical fartlek run is around an hour long, interspersed with some faster periods. The faster parts of the run are not structured, and the duration and speed are entirely up to the runner, as is the rest interval in between. The point of a fartlek run is to introduce speedwork in a fun and less structured way. This is a good workout for off-season speedwork.

Steady state runs: Steady state runs usually have a 5K race pace plus a minute to a minute and a half. This pace is in between an easy run pace and a threshold run pace. Why do it? It's more effective at increasing mitochondrial density and capillarization than a regular easy run. But remember: turning an easy run into a steady state run by running too fast defeats the purpose of a steady state run.

Every workout in a training plan is there for a reason, and each should be followed according to the plan. The interrelationship between all the workouts is crucial to successful running. If a runner runs their recovery run too quickly, they risk not being fully recovered for the next day's hard effort, thus compromising the more important hard workout.

Where to Run

Maybe your school is in a big city. Perhaps it's in the middle of nowhere. Either way, there are some basic principles that apply.

Follow basic traffic laws, especially if you're running on roads. Runners are supposed to run against traffic (cyclists ride with traffic). Obey traffic lights, look both ways before crossing the street, and be extra vigilant while running near traffic—because let's face it, drivers just aren't paying attention.

True story

One day at practice, my team had just done a workout on campus, and they were heading off campus for a two-mile cool down jog. There's an intersection at the main corner of campus. As the light turned green, the walk signal illuminated, and the team proceeded to cross the intersection in the crosswalk. Just then, a driver coming from the opposite direction turned left, toward the team. Many runners leaped out of the way, but two couldn't. One girl was hit and flew about fifty feet. The other girl went up and over the car, bouncing off the hood and roof and finally falling off. Luckily, neither was seriously hurt. Both insisted on racing that weekend, and I relented, although they were bruised and sore.

Running on roads is inherently dangerous. Running with earbuds in, makes it even more dangerous. Even running in places without cars can be more dangerous with earbuds in—there are animals out there that might want to sneak up on you. The two-legged animal (human) is the most dangerous. Don't let a human sneak up on you!

Running Tip #9: Never run with earbuds.

Also, when you're running off campus, remember that you're representing your team and your school. Have fun while training, but don't be hooligans in your community. Trust me, it will come back to bite you in the rear end.

True story

Way back when I ran high school cross-country, a group of us boys ran by the local Burger King. They had a life-size cardboard advertising thing out front of the restaurant, and we stole it and brought it to the school. We thought we were so smart, and cool. The problem was, it had snowed a little that morning, and the Burger King manager simply followed our footprints back to the school. We got in a heap of trouble!

Lastly, try to find grassy surfaces like parks, golf courses, and cemeteries to run through. Yes, cemeteries can be great, soft, grassy places to run. Just be respectful while you're in there. If you can't find grass, find dirt. Dirt roads, dirt alleys, or dirt trails all work.

HIGH SCHOOL

Running Tip #10: Run most of your miles on soft surfaces.

Remember that third law of Newton: yes, we want that impact force coming into our bodies, but all that force over and over again is abusive. Your body can only take so much before something breaks. Grass and dirt surfaces are ideal; concrete is the worst possible running surface, and should be avoided as much as possible.

This is easy if you live in central Kansas and have endless miles of dirt roads or grassy fields to pick from, but it's harder if you live in an urban area full of asphalt roads and concrete sidewalks. Concrete is *the* worst possible surface to run on, because it's so hard. In fact, concrete is six times harder than other road surfaces like asphalt or macadam. To test this, try hitting an asphalt road with a hammer. Then, try the same thing on a concrete sidewalk. You'll leave a dent in an asphalt road; you'll nearly break the hammer on a concrete surface.

I tell my runners to never, ever run on concrete unless they have to. I encourage them to run through front yards rather than on the concrete sidewalks.

A common injury that runners of all abilities can get is patellar tendonitis. That's an agitation and swelling of the tendon right below your kneecap. It hurts a lot. Every single time a kid on my team got patellar tendonitis, I'd ask if they were running on sidewalks. One hundred percent of the time, they were running on sidewalks. Save your patellar tendons. Run on soft surfaces. Be creative with your route planning. Mapmyrun.com is a great resource to see where grassy and/or dirt surfaces are near your school or home.

True story

I have a seven-mile run through an urban city of one hundred seventy thousand people, which has less than one mile of hard surface and almost no concrete. The first half-mile has a mixture of road, a small park, some sidewalk, and a couple of front yards. Then I run through the front lawn of the county offices building, and then I hop over onto the grassy center track of an old trolley line for about two miles. The trolley line ends at a cemetery (gravel roads), which I run through for half a mile, and then I can go straight from

> *the cemetery, onto a golf course (grass) for a mile. I exit out the other side of the golf course into a large city park (grass) for another half mile. From there I have to run a quarter mile on a road, which leads over to a college campus. Two miles around the campus (mostly grass), and the last half-mile home is through lawns and down dirt alleys. A seven-miler, and less than one mile is hard surface.*

Cross-Training

For our purposes, cross training is any workout—besides running—that's done with the intent to improve your running. A great example is weight lifting. Other examples are plyometrics, swimming, biking, using an elliptical machine, and hiking.

Cross training is also a great way to maintain fitness while recovering from an injury, and it's often part of rehabilitation. I've coached kids through the years who struggled a little with all the mileage involved with cross-country. No problem—I just had them switch out a few runs each week with swimming or biking. They still got a decent workout, and their legs weren't so beat up. And, they stayed injury-free.

Weight Training

I do want to spend some time talking about the weight room. Maybe you're from a really small school, and you're laughing because there is no weight room. Or, perhaps your school has a weight room, but it has nothing but squat platforms for the football team. Hopefully you have access to some sort of weight program, because resistance training (lifting), especially for teenage girls, is extremely helpful for middle or high school distance runners.

What exercises should you do? Well, try to focus on exercises that develop strength in the muscle groups that you use while running. Sorry boys, but the bench press will not make you run faster. It develops the central and lower parts of the pectoral muscles, and you don't use them while running. So, don't waste you're time with push-ups. The obvious big hitters for what to train are your legs (every muscle), your shoulders, and your core.

How much weight should you lift and how many reps and sets should you do? Old-school thinking was to lift lighter weight with high reps and many sets. That kind of weight lifting—with many small stimuli—isn't very different than running itself. The act of running is a series of tiny stimuli, repeated many, many times. The current theory is to lift heavier weights with fewer reps (five to six) and fewer sets (two to three).

Avoid max lifting. It trashes your muscles for days, doesn't enhance your running ability, and has a higher risk of injury. Similarly, don't weight train on heavy running days or after a race. Let your body rest and repair itself.

Running Tip #11: Never run with weights attached to any part of your body.

Weight vests, hand weights, and weights that attach to your ankles are bad for running—especially the weights that attach to your ankles. Remember, running works by you moving *forward*. Attaching weights to your body provides extra resistance in a *downward* direction. Extra downward resistance won't improve your ability to move forward—instead, once the weights are removed, it will make you bounce higher while running. If you want to use resistance while running forward, the resistance should be in a backward direction. There are running parachutes that provide this kind of backward resistance. These are reserved for elite sprinters, however, because these sprinters can actually run fast enough to deploy the chute behind them. Distance runners don't go fast enough. In short, attaching weights to yourself will alter your running form and potentially increase your risk of injury. Don't do it.

5

RACING

As I stated in the introduction, kids participate in cross-country for a myriad of reasons. Some love the racing part of it; some couldn't care less about racing or performance.

"Winning has nothing to do with racing. Most

days don't have races anyway. Winning is about struggle and effort and optimism, and never, ever, ever giving up." -Amby Burfoot

---

Whether you are or aren't really big on racing, you can't be on a cross-country team without racing occasionally. So, it would probably be helpful to explore some guidelines that will help you be more successful in races.

Let's break racing down into two pieces: racing strategy and racing tactics.

RACING STRATEGY:

How you're going to run this race.

Scenario #1: Externally focused strategy

You're racing a dual meet against a team that isn't very good. Your team desperately wants to sweep the top five places, and they expect you to be their fifth man. You know you have a really fast finish (your kick), so all you have to do to finish fifth is run with the other team's top guy and out-kick him at the finish.

This is your race strategy (a plan of how you're going to race), for this specific competition. It's an externally focused strategy because the race dynamics determine how you'll run this specific race.

Scenario #2: Internally focused strategy

You're racing in a very large, very competitive invitational. Based on your ability level, you're going to be running mid-pack in a field of up to two hundred runners. It will be really hard to find other kids from other teams, or even teammates, to try and pace off of. Therefore, your strategy for this race will be less focused on what's going on around you (you could move forward or backward twenty places and not really notice a difference), and more about what's going on within you as a runner. That is, you'll be focused on how you feel at different points of the race. This is an internally focused racing strategy.

Hypothetically, if you run the first mile conservatively, in mile two, if you're feeling good, you can start to pick up the pace a little (it always feels good to pass people), and then make the third mile your fastest. We already know you have a big kick, so your finish should be fast.

Some race strategies will revolve around the course, or even the weather. What if the course you're running has a crazy hill on it, for instance. Some hills are so ridiculously hard that they have their own evil names. Do you attack the hill hard, or do you run the hill moderately and then speed up over the top?

Or what if the wind is blowing forty miles per hour that race day and the course has little shelter from the wind. What would your race strategy be? For your team? For you individually?

True story

The day before my first cross-country race as a freshman in high school, my coach (the late, great Harry Gederman) sat all the newbies down and described how to run a 5K. He said, "When the gun goes off, you sprint your asses off, then you settle in and run the race, then you sprint your asses off to the finish." For a bunch of terrified newbies, this was great advice. It boiled the whole race down to two sprints and a run in between. It made the race a little less scary. Of course, this is a gross oversimplification of a high school 5K, but for a group of scared freshmen, it was gold.

Your coach will almost always have a strategy session with the team the day before a race. He or she will likely go over the course, the anticipated weather, and the competition, and have a team plan and individual plans for each team member. Often, these strategies will support each runner's strengths. If one runner is great at going out slowly and then passing everybody and winning, then that strategy will often be employed.

RACING TACTICS:

What you'll do during the race to support your strategy.

Let's go back to racing strategy scenario #1, where you have to be fifth man and out-sprint the first kid from the other team. Let's say on race day it's super windy. Your race tactics should include where to position yourself in the wind.

Your strategy in this scenario is simply to beat the first kid from the other team. It doesn't matter how fast or slow you run, just beat him. To make sure you conserve as much energy as possible so you can unleash that strong finishing kick, the smart tactic is to let the other guy break the wind, with you tucked in behind him. In windy conditions, the guy in front can use up to 20 percent more energy. So, let him exhaust himself in the wind.

This virtually ensures that at the end of the race, when it comes time for you to kick it in, you'll destroy the other guy, because he wasted all his energy running into the wind.

We had an expression on our team during windy races: "Don't be the idiot!" Don't be the person who runs in the wind and lets everyone else get the free ride in their draft.

True story

Once, after college, I ran a 10K in Colorado that offered four hundred dollars for first place and zero dollars for second place. Since the race was at a higher altitude (about sixty-five hundred feet) and the wind was really blowing (twenty to thirty miles per hour), nobody was setting a PR on this day. Everyone's strategy was similar: who cares about times, just win the four hundred dollars. My race strategy was to stay with the leaders and then use my very fast finishing kick to hopefully win first prize.

The course was set up so the first mile ran slightly downhill along a river, with the wind at our backs. Then the course crossed the river and went three straight miles into a huge headwind. Then, of course, it crossed back over the river and the last two miles were with a tailwind.

After we crossed the river at the mile mark, there were two of us in the lead by around fifteen seconds. The other guy put his head down and plowed through the headwind (with me right behind him) for about a minute or so. He then moved aside and gestured that I take my turn in front so he could get behind me and recover from his turn at the front. His idea was that we could take turns breaking the wind—that way, nobody else could catch us.

I laughed at this idea and refused to run in front, into the headwind. The other runner indicated that if we worked together, we could outdistance the group of five other guys right behind us. He was right, but if I spent half of the next three miles running in the headwind, I might be too tired to use my kick, and I'd miss out on the four hundred dollars. The prize money was all that mattered. It didn't matter how fast or slow we went.

So, the other runner, realizing that breaking the wind for the next three miles wasn't good for his chances at the four hundred dollars either, started jogging slowly, in an effort to force me to share the lead with him.

I politely informed him that I didn't care if the chase group caught up because I would outkick

> *them as well. This infuriated the other runner— he knew he couldn't beat my finishing kick. He now understood that his only chance to win was to run as hard as he could into the headwind, and hopefully I wouldn't be able to stay with him.*
>
> *But I did stay with him. We crossed back over the river and he was so spent from running as hard as he could in the headwind that when it came time for the finish, I easily outkicked him for the four hundred dollars. He was not happy.*

Other racing tactics might include what surfaces to run on. Say a section of a race course has a road alongside a surface with poor traction. If you're allowed to race on either, race on the road. Better traction, harder surface.

What if the race day is hot (ninety degrees and sunny)? It might be beneficial to seek the shady side of the course and try to stay as cool as possible in those conditions.

Often before an important race, a cross-country team reviews critical feature of the course and how to run them. Sections of questionable footing, sharp turns, uphills, downhills, water, etc.

Famous Hills with Names

When hills have names, you should be a little scared. Here are some examples:

- Zigzag Hill – my home middle school course
- Heartbreak Hill - Boston Marathon Course
- Parachute Hill – Belmont Plateau, Philadelphia
- Sure Kill Hill – Belmont Plateau, Philadelphia
- Cardiac Hill – Sunken Meadow, Long Island
- Little Willis Hill – NPEC, Colorado Springs
- Big Willis Hill – NPEC, Colorado Springs
- Bear Cage Hill – Franklin Park, Boston
- Eliminator Hill – Monte Vista, California
- Widowmaker Hill – East Valley, Spokane

6

STRETCHING

The term "stretching" has meant a number of things over the past hundred years. We've had ballistic stretching, static stretching, active isolated stretching, and dynamic "stretching" (drills), to name the biggies.

The purpose of stretching is to lengthen the muscle being stretched. But before we go too far, let's examine that idea. Is lengthening muscles even a good idea? It was long assumed that longer muscles are better muscles. This is actually rarely true. The power that your muscles produce depends on the length of those muscles—and each muscle has an optimal length that will produce maximal power. If it's too long, or too short, it has less power. You want muscles that are just right.

Think of a gymnast who suddenly wants to be a distance runner. That gymnast will be incredibly flexible. Is she more powerful as a distance runner just because her muscles are longer? No. In fact, she's likely weaker with regards to the specific demands of distance running.

There are times, however, when a muscle is too short and really does need to be lengthened in order to produce more power. Distance runners require a fairly small range of motion for our leg muscles. This means that you don't need the flexibility to be able to palm the floor when you touch your toes—being able to simply touch your ankles is almost always good enough. So, since distance runners don't need really long muscles, you probably don't need to stretch them into longer muscles.

Static Stretching

Static stretching is what most people refer to as stretching. Typical static stretching involves manipulating your body into a position that elicits a stretching sensation in a specific muscle, and then holding that position for a period of time—typically fifteen to thirty seconds.

Static stretching has fallen out of favor for a number of reasons. If your coach still has your team performing static stretching, you should politely indicate that that practice should change.

HIGH SCHOOL

The main reasons to not static stretch are fourfold.

1. It was believed that stretching reduces an athlete's chances of getting injured. This theory has been disproven: numerous studies (Small-2008, Thacker-2004, Amako-2003) from the 2000s showed that teams that static stretched and teams that didn't, all suffered the same injury rates.

2. Distance runners rarely need longer muscles.

3. Let's assume that a runner really does need to lengthen a muscle. The way static stretching is typically performed does nothing to permanently lengthen the muscle: to actually see a change in muscle length, the athlete must hold the stretching position for a minimum of three to five minutes, multiple times a day. Stretching a muscle for fifteen seconds does absolutely nothing to change the length of a muscle in the long term.

4. Most importantly, numerous studies (Yamaguchi-2005, McNeal-2003 and Marek 2005) have shown that static stretching *reduces power* by anywhere from 3 to 10 percent. If you static stretch before your race, you'll start the race less powerful than if you did nothing. It doesn't take a running expert to realize that reduced power for a race is a bad idea.

Dynamic "Stretching," or Drills

Dynamic drills are a series of short movements that help prepare the muscles for the rigors of racing through repetitive movement. They aren't really stretching at all—instead, they focus on the range of motion in the specific muscles used for running. They increase heart rate, blood flow, and body temperature. In short, they're the best way to get your muscles ready to run.

Examples of dynamic drills include: butt kicks, leg swings, toy soldiers, cat/cow, pike stretches, and hacky sacks. Almost all teams across the nation do some version of dynamic drills before a race. Your team's version may be different than the next team's, but they all aim to do the same thing: they prepare your body to race without reducing its power.

7

FOOD AND SUPPLEMENTS

Consider your body to be similar to a car engine: the better the fuel, the better the performance. As you develop as a runner, you'll graduate from a cheap, entry-level car into a highly tuned racecar. A racecar will run on low-octane gas, but poorly—it must have the best fuel to perform at its best.

Your body is no different. The old adage, "garbage in, garbage out," holds true. The better the fuel you put into your engine, the better your body will perform. Aside from your regular training, it's your diet that has the greatest impact on your performance. If you eat a terrible diet, it won't matter how hard you practice every day, you'll be limited by your poor diet. You can't out-train your diet.

Look, I get it. You're a teenager. You're going to eat some fast food. Pizza is yummy. Soda tastes great. These are fine in small quantities, once in a while. Just have them as a treat, not as every meal.

One of the best ways to ensure that you're eating well is to actually cook. Be responsible for cooking for your whole family one day a week. Studies show that kids who cook are more aware of ingredients and food quality than those who don't.

Whenever I travel with my cross-country team, we always eat in. Whether it's during team camp in the mountains or going to cross-country meets (we rent houses on Airbnb), we grocery shop and cook together. This makes everyone responsible for the good nourishment of the team.

There are literally thousands of diets out there-some work, some don't. There are so many theories on this nutrient versus that nutrient, this food versus that food, that it can make you dizzy. In just the past thirty years alone, carbohydrates have been both glorified and demonized. The same goes for fats. The truth is, they're both important.

Understanding how the human body works is also very important: how your body consumes calories and what it does with them; how different fuel sources are stored for use in the body, and in the muscles specifically. There are tons of books available on exercise physiology and how the body utilizes energy. We don't have time for that here. And, again, you're a teenager; so let's take a realistic approach to your overall diet.

BASICS OF A GOOD DIET:

This section could be a hundred pages long, but for the sake of sanity, I'll just go over the key points.

The number one thing to remember when it comes to your diet is to try and minimize processed foods. What are processed foods? Pretty much anything that's been prepared somewhere else. Eating out is a simple example, but a lot of the things you can buy at the supermarket are processed. Microwave dinners are processed, for example — avoid anything that needs to be microwaved.

Try to eat food in a form as close as possible to its natural state. Hot Cheetos aren't found in nature unless someone dropped some in the woods.

Eating right isn't rocket science. Keep the food simple (bread shouldn't have thirty ingredients), original (minimally processed), and varied (boatloads of fruits and veggies, dairy, meat, grains, and nuts and seeds).

Sugar

Immediately following a race, a hard workout, or a long run, a sugary treat is actually a good idea. Your body wants to return to its original state as quickly as possible. Since you've

depleted the sugar from those muscles, along with water, getting sugar back into your muscles as soon as possible speeds recovery for the next day. In general though, your body doesn't need or want refined sugar.

True story

Every two years, I do a little experiment with my team. We call it the Skittles run. Skittles are basically pure sugar, with a little color and flavoring. They're pure refined sugar. We do this experiment on a Monday, where the workout would be a short, easy run, let's say four miles. Each team member gets a handful of Skittles, or about two hundred to three hundred calories' worth. They all eat their Skittles and wait for twenty minutes. Then they run the four miles. Every kid comes back from their run and declares that they've never felt so awful on a run, never mind just a simple four-miler. Some veteran varsity runners have even reported that they had to walk a portion of their run after eating the Skittles.

"But wait, I thought sugar is energy?" you may be asking. And you'd be right. But how it's delivered to the muscles is important. During that twenty-minute wait after consuming the Skittles, a chain reaction happens in the body. First, our stomachs quickly send a message to our brains that we just ate a ton of sugar, and then our stomachs quickly digest the sugar and send it straight into our bloodstream. This is the sugar high. The problem is, our brains don't like our blood sugar getting too high. So then our bodies release a bunch of insulin, which rapidly forces that blood sugar level down. Too far down. This is the sugar low.

Low blood sugar is what marathoners experience when they "hit the wall." We just creatively reproduced the sensation through the manipulation of insulin. Most kid's claim that the Skittles run was so awful, they'd never do it again.

There are so many healthier options for calories than refined sugar. The sugars found naturally in fruits and vegetables are fine. Stick with those!

What to Eat and What not to Eat

I'd highly recommend checking out the book *Food Rules: An Eater's Manual*, by Michael Pollan, from your local library. It's short and can be read in about an hour, but it has words of wisdom that should last a lifetime. An example of one of his "rules" is the following: "It's not food if it arrived through the window of your car." Remember this whenever you pull up to a drive-through!

Similarly, no matter what you pack for lunch, it's probably a better option than your school's lunch, and certainly a better option than getting fast food or hitting up a convenience store. Doritos and Mountain Dew will make you feel—and run—like garbage three hours later at practice.

Carbo-Loading

There is no need whatsoever for carbohydrate loading (carbo-loading) before a 5K. Yes, that's right: avoid the big pasta dinners the night before races. Really, carbo-loading only works for events longer than around eighteen miles. In fact, carbo-loading will likely impair 5K performance.

So how does carbo-loading work, and why is it bad for a 5K runner? Let's use the car metaphor again. Assume that you want to drive from Boston to Washington D.C.: that's four hundred forty miles. Your car can only carry enough fuel to go four hundred miles. You aren't going to make it to D.C., are you?

Your body is the same when you're running a marathon. Some people have enough carbs to make it 26.2 miles just fine, but many don't have enough carbs to make it the full marathon distance. So, to make sure they make it to the finish line, they carbo-load a couple of days before the race. By eating a ton of carbs in the twenty-four hours leading up to a marathon, their body temporarily stores extra carbs, and that's usually enough to make it to the finish line. Carbo-loading doesn't make them go any faster; it just extends the distance they can run without having to stop for more fuel.

Now let's look at what carbo-loading would do for a 5K. Still using the car metaphor, extra gas means extra weight. This will hurt gas mileage and fuel efficiency as the car drives along. We're talking about the same thing with carbo-loading for your body—an extra pound correlates to a ten-seconds slower over a 5K distance.

When you carbo-load, you're adding not only the weight of the extra carbs, but also the weight of the extra water required to hold those carbs in place inside your muscles. (And the extra water weight is six times the extra weight of the carbs.)

To summarize, you don't need extra carbs to run a 5K: you already have enough carbs to run at least eighteen to twenty miles before you run out. Carbo-loading for a 5K will just weigh you down and make you run slower.

Energy Gels

Never, ever, use an energy gel unless you're in the last six miles of a marathon. They're marketed as "energy," but all they do is mess with your blood sugar and the hormones regulating it. Remember, you have eighteen to twenty miles' worth of carbs in you already. You don't need to eat extra before or during the race. In no way can an energy gel improve your 5K performance.

Vitamins and Minerals

Pretty much every kid in America should be taking a daily multivitamin. All the processed foods we eat are so devoid of basic nutrition, despite being fortified, that a multivitamin is necessary to fill in the gaps where our diets aren't supplying adequate nutrients.

Iron

This is important! In chapter 9, I go into great detail about why iron is vital. Low iron will lead to runner's anemia. You do not want this.

OVER-THE-COUNTER (OTC) MEDICATIONS

Painkillers, Anti-Inflammatories, NSAIDs

Ibuprofen (the main ingredient in Advil and Motrin) is a common non-steroidal anti-inflammatory drug, or NSAID. It can act as an anti-inflammatory, and can be a great help in certain situations. Generally speaking, however, ibuprofen offers a short-term benefit, but is a long-term detriment. That means you shouldn't take ibuprofen daily. Take it every once in a while for an acute inflammation issue, and then stop taking it. Constant usage of NSAIDs diminishes the body's ability to naturally heal itself, according to a 2013 Corso study.

Antihistamines

Whether generic or brand name, you really don't want to be taking antihistamines, except maybe right before bedtime (especially if you have the flu). What do they do? Well, they dry up a runny nose, watery eyes, and stop the sneezing. They're popular for sufferers of seasonal allergies, but they have a lot of side effects, including drowsiness, fatigue, muscle soreness, and muscle cramps. That doesn't sound like what we want to experience for running. Antihistamines last for about four to six hours in the body. So, avoid them for six hours before running. You won't die if your nose runs. Just use a Kleenex!

Decongestants

These are the pills that clear up your stuffy nose. There are a few different active ingredients that qualify as decongestants. One of them, pseudoephedrine, is banned by all anti-doping entities (WADA, USADA, NCAA, NAIA, and your state high school governing body). If the active ingredient of your decongestant is pseudoephedrine, it's banned. Don't risk it. Just take a different decongestant that's legal.

Pseudoephedrine is banned because it's just a little too potent. It's both a bronchodilator (it opens up all the tubing in your lungs), and a central nervous system stimulant (it amps you up, like caffeine).

8

WATER AND HYDRATION

How much water does the human body need? How much water do you need to optimize your running? There are some different theories out there. The one we hear the most is that you should drink as much water as possible and stay hydrated at all costs. Another theory is that you actually perform even better when you're fairly dehydrated. Yet another theory is that you should simply drink when you're thirsty. There are numerous studies that support each of these ideas, but some of them are thrown in our faces a little more.

Let's look at water and why you need it. Water is important for survival, and it's important for running. There are whole books devoted to water and athletic performance. In general, better hydration leads to improved bodily functions. Your blood doesn't get too thick, you sweat more effectively and dissipate heat, and the chemical reactions in your cells are more efficient.

But water also has a drawback: it's heavy. Carrying around extra water during a race costs time. In a 5K, one pound equals roughly ten seconds or so.

So how do you measure this tradeoff? Where is that sweet spot where you're hydrated enough, but not overly so? Well, it's a little different for everyone.

Have you ever watched a world-class marathon? Notice how elite runners barely drink during the race. They'll drink somewhere between ten to twenty ounces of fluid during the 26.2 mile race, and yet, depending on weather conditions, they'll lose 3 to 8 percent of their body weight through sweat. And remarkably, these elite athletes are often running faster at the end of the race than at the beginning. This is a perfect example of the tradeoff of hydration. These runners are up to ten to twelve pounds lighter at the finish, which allows them to run faster, but they're pretty dehydrated.

True story

I knew an elite racer back in the 90s who would deliberately dehydrate herself two to three pounds before a 5K. Was this smart? Maybe, maybe not. I know another elite runner from that time who claimed that before a marathon, he liked to feel like a cargo plane loaded for takeoff. Was this smart? Maybe, maybe not. Both were elite runners both had a differing approach to race preparation with regards to hydration. Personally, I've lost over a gallon (eight pounds) of sweat while running ... and finished fast.

9

INJURIES AND MALADIES

Once you become a runner, there's nothing worse than not being able to run. As a beginner, this just sounds like crazy talk, but trust me, there's nothing more maddening that being unable to run.

Distance runners are the most injured athletes in high school. The average high school girl who runs cross-country and distance for track will get injured, on average, twenty-four times during her four-year high school career, and boys will get injured eighteen times, according to a fifteen year, Washington State study by Rauh, et al.

But what constitutes an injury? For the Washington study, it was defined as anything that causes you to not be able to practice for three or more days. They went further, and defined injuries by the length of time that they missed practice for. A minor injury meant the athlete couldn't run for three to ten days, a mid-level injury meant no running for ten to thirty days, and a major injury was over thirty days of no running. For the average girl who gets injured twenty-four times in four years, eighteen of her injuries were minor, four were mid-level, and two were major. The average boy had fourteen minor injuries, three mid-level, and one major.

You will get injured as a distance runner. I've only known *one* athlete who went the duration of high school and never missed a day of practice. Running miles and miles is abusive to your body (especially if you aren't recovering every night and eating well), and the cumulative effect of that abuse is that eventually something fails.

When I read the results of the Washington study, I thought the injury rates they listed were far too high. Luckily, I still have my training logs from high school. I leafed through them and recorded all the times I missed three-plus days of practice for some ailment or another. I totaled sixteen times, with a minor/mid-level/major breakdown of thirteen/two/one. So, my personal injury rates were not that different from the study results. What struck me is that I fancied myself a fairly healthy and durable runner back in high school. Apparently I was just average.

Improvement as a runner happens in tiny increments every single day, and injuries get in the way of that progress. Each day we work out, we get just a little better than we were the day before. Getting injured and taking time off to heal means you're not getting better that day. And when you add up all the days that the average high school runner misses due to an injury, that's a lot of missed days of practice, which means a lot of missed days to become a better athlete. Half of success in high school and in college is simply staying healthy.

"Your body provides you with constant feedback that can help improve your running performance while minimizing biomechanical stress. Learn to differentiate between the discomfort of effort and the pain of injury. When you practice listening, you increase competence in persevering through the former and responding with respect and compassion to the latter." -Gina Greenlee

---

Running Tip #12: Let your coach know immediately when something doesn't feel right.

If your coach or trainer is knowledgeable about injuries, have them take a look at it. Remember, the worst torture for a runner is not being able to run.

Running injuries aren't like injuries in other sports. Runners don't typically tear their ACL, break bones, or suffer other traumatic injuries. No, running injuries are much more subtle. They are overuse injuries that often develop over weeks. Most injuries can be caught early and managed, before they become the kinds of problems that cause you to miss practice.

Your garden-variety running injury initially presents during or after a run, where something just feels a little "off." The average runner shrugs it off and keeps training. This is a mistake. The little something that was "off" gets a little more "off" each day, until eventually it's getting in the way of running. Now it's a full blown injury. Had the runner noted the issue before it was an injury; it could've likely been managed and healed without missing practice time.

INJURIES:

Blisters

Blisters are caused by excessive friction on the skin's surface. The brain tries to protect the skin by injecting fluid in between the outer two layers of skin. The blister itself is a defensive measure by the body.

Treatment: Pop the blister bubble using a safety pin and drain all the fluid out. When popping the blister, don't just make a pinhole because it may reseal and redevelop as a blister again. Instead, try to make a small slash or incision. Once drained, the blister should feel much better.

> **Running Tip #13: The best thing to place over a blister is duct tape.**

Never put a Band-Aid over a blister and then go for a run. The Band-Aid will likely move around, not cover the original blister, and cause a new blister because it's rubbing somewhere else. Duct tape won't move. Remember, blisters are caused by excessive friction. Duct tape is slippery (on the non-sticky side). This eliminates the friction problem. Just leave the duct tape on there for a few days—after a few days, the under layer of skin will have toughened up and the duct tape can be removed with no further blister issues. The nice thing about the human body is its adaptability. It recognizes that the area that got the blister might be prone to getting more blisters. So when that outer layer of skin comes off (like it's supposed to), the under layer will become thicker and more resistant to getting another blister.

Shin Splints

In distance runners, shin splints are located in the soft-tissue area just to the inside of the shin bone.

There are a lot of old wives' tales about what causes shin splints. Some will say it's from flat feet. It isn't. Some will say it's from your shoes. It isn't. Shoe-insert companies will say that certain inserts can cure shin splints. They can't.

Shin splints in distance runners are ultimately caused by a muscle imbalance between three muscles: the posterior tibialis (deep, lower calf) versus the anterior tibialis (upper outside shin) and peroneus brevis (lower outside shin). The posterior tibialis becomes really strong really quickly in beginning runners. The other two muscles that are supposed to keep that muscle in balance are slower to develop. As a result, we have a muscle imbalance. The posterior tibialis is now free to get in trouble, and it actually tears away from the tibia. This causes all kinds of inflammation and pain.

Treatment: Ice helps reduce the inflammation and subsequently the pain, but doesn't fix the problem of the muscle imbalance. NSAIDs like ibuprofen (Motrin, Advil, etc.) also help to reduce inflammation and ease the pain, but again, they don't solve the problem.

The anterior tibialis and the preens brevis must be strengthened to get the muscle balance back. Backward running and duck walks (walking with your heels down and your forefeet off the ground) usually accomplish this.

Curing shin splints will take some time. It took weeks to develop them, and it will take a couple of weeks to completely cure them. As a new runner, if you walk like a duck a couple of times a day for a minute or so, you'll never get shin splints.

True story

My wife's high school coach had the entire track team run a full lap on the track backward every single day. They did this to start practice. This practice greatly reduced the incidence of shin splints.

Tendonitis

The two tendons that typically cause problems in distance runners are the Achilles tendon and the patellar tendon. Patellar tendonitis is far more common, and this tendon is located right below the kneecap. It connects your kneecap with your shinbone (tibia). A healthy patellar tendon can be aggressively massaged (with your thumb or a pencil eraser) and it should feel awkward and a little ticklish. If there is any pain or discomfort at all, you're getting, or already have tendonitis. Since there are no pain sensors in tendons and ligaments, the pain felt by the runner is from the surrounding inflammation. Tendonitis in either tendon can put you out of commission for days or even weeks. Be aware of your body and notify your coach immediately if you feel discomfort in either tendon.

Treatment: Using ice and/or ibuprofen to reduce the inflammation helps to ease the pain in the short term, but fails to cure the underlying issue. Ultimately, cross-friction massage is the best way to solve the root cause. Treat the tendon before running by icing it and then massaging it rigorously in a crossways direction with the leg fully extended. The massage won't be pleasant—an aggressive cross-friction massage should be somewhat painful. The rule of thumb is that if this massage doesn't hurt, you don't have tendonitis.

True story

In college, I developed a nasty case of patellar tendonitis in both of my knees. This was probably because I attended an urban college and was running far too much on concrete, which strongly contributes to patellar tendonitis. So, I had to get the tendonitis massaged with the painful cross-friction method. I would hobble (because walking was painful) into the training room before practice for my treatment. There was one trainer (a diabolical woman with platinum-white hair) who took particular delight in torturing me. We both knew that the more vicious the massage, the more effective it would be. So, she gave me a wooden dowel to bite down on while she used a number 2 pencil eraser on my patellar tendon for ten minutes. Some days I swear that I nearly blacked out from the pain. But after ten minutes of torture, I could get out there and run ten miles with little pain. This lasted for five to six weeks and eventually got better.

This injury requires this specific treatment or it will take forever to go away. As you're sitting in class, probably bored out of your mind, simply get your thumb into that tendon and massage it for five minutes, a few times a day, and the tendonitis will slowly go away. The same treatment goes for the Achilles tendon. The only difference is you'll have to point your toes downward like a ballerina.

Plantar Fasciitis

This is the fascia on the bottom of your foot. Pain typically manifests on the front of your heel and radiates forward toward the forefoot. Fascias are a lot like tendons, and treatment is similar.

Treatment: Ice and massage. Massaging a fascia is performed in any direction. The best way to do this is with a golf ball. Put the golf ball on the ground and roll your foot around on top of it. Be careful to avoid rolling the golf ball directly under the "hot spot" just in front of the heel. The rest of the mid-foot and forefoot are fair game, though. This is another treatment that you can do right in class. If your classroom has a tile floor, you'll want to wait, however. It's hard to stop the golf ball from slipping out from under your foot and rolling across the classroom. You don't want your teacher to confiscate your treatment tool.

Iliotibial Band Syndrome (ITBS)

The iliotibial, or IT, band is another fascia, and it's located on the side of the thigh. It connects to the outside of the top of the tibia with the gluteus maximus at the other end. There are a lot of things (overuse issues) that can lead to IT problems. Pain almost always manifests on the outside of the knee—that seems to be the weak link that gets in trouble.

Treatment: Stretching the gluteus maximus helps a lot. Great relief can be found with a foam roller or massage stick. Massaging the IT band is unpleasant. Really unpleasant. Even rolling out a healthy IT band on a roller is somewhat unpleasant! Notice that the girl in the photo is putting on the grimace smile.

MALADIES:

Be mindful of your body. Be aware of how your legs and muscles normally feel. Then, when something feels "off," let your coach know right away.

Influenza (The Flu)

There are three important things to know about the flu and how it relates to running: the flu shot, when to and when not to run, and how to keep the flu out of your lungs.

The flu shot: According to the Centers for Disease Control and Prevention (CDC), the flu shot reduces your odds of getting the flu by around 60 percent, but this varies from year to year as the strains of influenza change. So, should you get a flu shot every year? That's a personal decision made by you and your parents. If you choose to get the flu shot, try to do it before the cross-country season starts or after it ends—sometimes it can cause minor body aches or a low-grade fever for a couple of days. The flu shot can't give you the flu, however (this is a common misconception). The flu shot does contain some nasty chemicals that you may not want to put into your body. Educate yourself first.

When to run and when not to run: The flu isn't fun, and you'll likely feel its effects for seven to ten days. You only have to avoid running for about forty-eight hours, though. Our bodies are pretty good at fighting the flu, and our immune systems know exactly what to do in order to get rid of it: hike up our internal thermostat for a couple of days and kill it. This is why you run a high fever for a couple of days—the flu can't survive that little bit of extra heat.

Running Tip #14: Never run if you have a fever.

A fever is your body's way of "cooking" the flu to death.

Your body is already working its hardest during this time, so don't push it by running while you have a fever.

Once your fever goes away, that tells you that your body knows that the flu has been killed and eradicated from your body. The problem is that all the other after-effects (stuffy nose, congestion, and that awesome cough) linger for days and even weeks. You can run once the fever is done—you're technically not sick with the flu anymore. It takes a few days or weeks for your body to purge all that extra fluid from your nasal cavity and lungs, however. This extra time is just an annoyance, though, and can be run through.

How to keep the flu out of your lungs: From a runner's perspective, you can run just fine with a number of symptoms. Perhaps you have a runny nose? You can run with that. Or maybe you have a stuffy nose and congestion? You can run just fine with both of those. But what about a nasty cough? Well, you can run, but it will be painful and annoying.

All that fluid in your lungs that you're painfully hacking up for a week or two after the flu will impair performance by clogging up your lungs. This is a bad thing, and it can be prevented: the trick is to keep fluid from getting into your lungs in the first place by taking an over-the-counter antihistamine before you go to bed. They'll dry you out and help you sleep. By doing this, you greatly reduce the amount of fluid that gets into your lungs, and you won't have to painfully hack it all back out of your lungs for three weeks.

Runner's Anemia

Also called iron deficiency anemia, runner's anemia is by far the most common malady to affect distance runners. It's estimated that two-thirds to three quarters of female high school cross-country runners suffer from this, and up to one quarter of boys do as well. And many don't even know they have it.

Every distance runner in America should be taking an iron supplement—the only exception to this rule is if you have a genetic condition called hemochromatosis. But why is iron so important, and why are distance runners more in need of it than anyone else? Iron has many functions in the body, and the main function is in the making of red blood cells. These red blood cells are what carry oxygen from your lungs to your muscles. So, for a runner, red blood cells are pretty important. The problem is that running is fairly abusive to blood cells: you literally damage blood cells in the bottoms of your feet with every stride. At night, while you sleep, your liver inspects every blood cell and discards any that are damaged. So, your runner body is constantly forced into making a lot of fresh new blood cells every day. This puts a very large demand on the iron stores in your body.

Without enough iron to work with in your body, your brain becomes forced to prioritize where to use its limited supply of iron, and it prioritizes making red blood cells. Well, that's a good thing for a runner, right? The answer is yes and no. One place it will underprioritize iron utilization is in making certain enzymes. One of these enzymes in particular is the catalyst for burning sugar in your muscles. So, if your iron gets too low, you start to lose the ability to burn sugar in your muscles.

This is not good for a 5K runner. Sure, your muscles can burn fat as their fuel source, but fat burns slower, and slower is how you'll race. This is "runner's anemia," and you don't want it! It takes months to dig yourself into this iron-depleted hole, and it takes months to dig yourself out of it. Avoid the hole altogether by taking an iron supplement.

Symptoms: The symptoms of runner's anemia will start with your race times getting a little slower. Then, as it progresses, you'll have trouble with the end of long runs and your hard workouts will become exhausting. Next, you'll notice that all of your runs are overly fatiguing, you're racing like garbage, and you're tired when you wake up in the morning. If it continues, you really can't run much at all anymore: racing becomes a pipe dream, and fatigue is overwhelming. Ancillary symptoms include depression and anxiety.

Diagnosis: You'll need to get a blood test to check your ferritin level. Ferritin is a protein that binds to the iron in your blood. But keep in mind that what's listed as the "normal" range for ferritin simply doesn't work for an endurance athlete—especially not a runner. The bottom of the medical "normal" range for ferritin is twelve—but that's for couch potatoes. Anything under thirty for a girl and fifty for a boy is cause for concern, and will likely begin to impair performance.

Solution: Take an iron supplement. Your local grocery store will probably have numerous choices—the ones that seem to work best for distance runners are chelated iron. Get any brand; just be sure it's chelated. If your iron levels get really, really low, there is a liquid iron cocktail sold under the brand name Floridix. It's found at many health stores nationwide. Floridix is more potent than the pill form, and works more effectively at increasing ferritin levels.

Caution: Runner's anemia is a term that your physician will likely not recognize. When they hear the word anemia, they'll check two blood measurements: hemoglobin and hematocrit. With runner's anemia, both of those markers will likely be inside "normal" ranges. So, you're interested in one number only: the ferritin number. Again, it should be over thirty for girls and over fifty for boys.

True story

Years ago I coached a girl who developed a nasty case of runner's anemia. At first, her race times started to slip. Then she started having trouble finishing workouts. Eventually, running itself was hard, and she passed out a couple of times while running. I immediately recognized what

HIGH SCHOOL

was happening: she was digging the iron-deficiency hole. I reached out to her parents to get a blood test done and get an accurate ferritin reading. They took her to the doctor. The doctor had no clue as to what runner's anemia was, and dismissed it. Her ferritin count was four. The doctor instead diagnosed her with a heart condition. The girl's parents trusted the diagnosis of the doctor over the track coach. They began a series of invasive tests that took months to complete and cost the family a significant amount of money. After all those tests and all that money, the doctor concluded that she didn't have a heart condition after all, but couldn't figure out why she was so fatigued and passing out. All along I pleaded to just give the poor girl some iron. Finally, after the doctor had given up, the parents agreed and got her some of the Floridix liquid iron supplement. She improved immediately, was back to running within a week, and has been fine since. She still doesn't have a heart condition.

10

OTHER IMPORTANT STUFF

Sleep

Do you get stronger while you're running? Do you get stronger in the weight room? The answer is no. You get stronger hours later.

You get stronger while you sleep: this is when your body repairs itself from the rigors of the day. You literally tear your muscles to shreds while running. It takes time—downtime—to repair all the damage you've done during the day. This is why sleep is so vitally important to being a good runner. Inadequate sleep equals inadequate recovery. It leaves you tired for the next workout and can develop into a dangerous cycle.

Teenagers have the second-highest sleep requirement of any age group: only newborn babies need more sleep. The average teenager requires nine hours of sleep per night. But you're not average—you're an athlete. That means your sleep requirements are even higher. You might be thinking, "Yeah, I'd sleep all day, but the whole school thing gets in the way of that." Make time to sleep. If you're exhausted and tired all the time, how can you be an effective runner?

True story

I coached a girl a few years ago who really valued the importance of a good night's sleep. Her theory was that if she were well rested, she would be a better student, runner, and person. So, she went to bed at ten o'clock every night. It didn't matter if her homework was done or not. It didn't matter if she studied for that quiz or not. Ten o'clock, every night. You might be thinking that this early bedtime would hurt her grades. After all, she's going to bed without studying or finishing her homework sometimes! The reality was that she was more efficient at everything she did, and her time-management skills were also extraordinary because she was well rested. She was a state qualifier in both cross-country and track, and she was also class valedictorian.

Human Growth Hormone (HGH)

This could be the most important hormone in the human body. It's responsible for many functions important to distance running, including recovery speed and tissue building. The brain releases it during sleep, but not until about ninety minutes into a restful sleep. The release of HGH tapers off around three hours into sleep. It's said that Einstein took numerous naps each day, greatly increasing his HGH production. If you have the opportunity to take a nice nap after a long run, by all means do it.

Pre-Race Poor Sleep

Don't worry if you have a fitful night's rest on the night before a race. Sleep is a cumulative benefit that works off what we would consider a moving average. If you've had a great week of sleep, then one poor night won't affect race performance.

Massage

Massage is extremely beneficial if done correctly. Massage helps to break up scar tissue, increases blood flow, and realigns muscles. All of these are helpful for any athlete.

The best kind of massage for cross-country runners is sports massage. There are many types of massage, but to realize the benefits spoken of already, the massage must be reasonably deep. If performed properly, it shouldn't be a pleasant experience.

A good massage therapist, if visited regularly, gets to know the idiosyncrasies of your body, your legs, and your muscles. They'll be able to detect issues that might lead to an injury someday and work to remediate the issue before it becomes a problem. For six years I was on the massage table every Sunday night. I honestly believe that my massage therapist kept me mostly injury-free and on my feet for that time.

Since a good sports massage is somewhat stressful on the body, a massage should always be performed before an easy day on the training schedule. Never ever get a massage within the thirty-six hours before you have to race.

You might be thinking, "I'm just a kid trying to run cross-country. Do I really need a massage therapist?" No, you don't, but you should at least try to realize some of these benefits on your own if massage isn't an option. A twenty-dollar investment in a massage stick, or my new favorite company, GoFit. They make a ton of self massage tools. You can even make your own massage stick out of PVC tubing from a hardware store.

Hot and Cold Water

If you happen to have some tight leg muscles, a pre-run leg soak in hot water could help loosen those muscles up a little, but at the expense of your legs feeling lethargic and like Jell-O. Similarly, fully submersing yourself in a hot tub feels great, but does nothing to improve performance or recovery. Hot baths can be used prior to running if only the legs are submerged, but they should not be used for at least four hours post-exercise, regardless of how good they feel.

Far more important to the distance runner is the "ice bath." Extended time in an ice bath (ten to thirty minutes depending on the water temperature) can also trigger what's known as a "flush." In short, when you're sitting in an ice bath, your brain constricts the blood vessels to the cold areas. After a while, however, it starts to worry about hypothermia and possibly losing a limb, so it suddenly dilates everything and increases your heart rate from around sixty beats per minute to about one hundred fifty beats per minute. The result is a flushing out of all the junk accumulated in the vascular system, which—you guessed it—speeds recovery.

Never use a ice bath prior to running—only after. The efficacy of cold baths is greatest when used after a strenuous workout, long run, or race. Both hot and cold baths are great once in a while, but shouldn't be used all the time.

THE 14 RUNNING TIPS

Please note that there could be an entire book of running tips. These are the ones that are especially pertinent to high school cross country runners, and are sometimes overlooked.

Running tip #1: It will be unpleasant at first.

Running tip #2: It gets easier.

Running tip #3: Your 100 percent effort never changes. You just get faster.

Running tip #4: Tie your shoes! And double-knot them!

Running tip #5: Your running shoes are not your everyday shoes.

Running tip #6: When it's cold and windy, always run *into* the wind (headwind) first, and *with* the wind (tailwind) on the way home.

THE 14 RUNNING TIPS

Running tip #7: Twisting your torso isn't swinging your arms.

Running tip #8: Warming up and cooling down are a lot more important than you think.

Running tip #9: Never run with earbuds.

Running tip #10: Run most of your miles on soft surfaces.

Running tip #11: Never run with weights attached to any part of your body.

Running tip #12: Let your coach know immediately when something doesn't feel right.

Running tip #13: The best thing to place over a blister is duct tape.

Running tip #14: Never run if you have a fever.

GLOSSARY

Acid buffering – also called anaerobic capacity, this is ability of the body, and the muscles in particular, to cope with the acidic environment created from extended anaerobic running.

Acid tolerance – the body's ability to tolerate the acidic by-products of anaerobic running.

Aerobic running – low- to moderate-intensity running where the oxygen requirements of the runner are met by the oxygen delivery system (lungs, heart, blood).

Anaerobic running – higher-intensity running where the oxygen requirements of the runner exceed the oxygen delivery system.

Adenosine triphosphate (ATP) – at the cellular level, this is the fuel that the mitochondria burn to produce energy.

GLOSSARY

Capillarization – the amount of tiny blood vessels that intertwine the muscles, delivering oxygen to them.

Carbohydrate loading (carbo-loading) – The practice of eating large quantities of carbohydrates the day before a marathon.

Concentric contraction – a muscle contracting while getting shorter.

Dorsiflexion – pointing your foot upwards.

Heel-toe drop – the difference between the height of your shoe's heel, and its forefoot.

Dynamic drills – a series of varied drills designed to prepare the body for running and racing.

Eccentric contraction – a muscle contracting while lengthening.

Human growth hormone (HGH) – an important hormone that helps recovery and many other bodily functions.

Iliotibial band syndrome (ITBS) – an agitation of the IT band, causing pain, typically on the outside of the knee.

Lactate – a by-product of anaerobic exercise.

Lactate threshold (LT) – also called the anaerobic threshold, this is the running speed at which the runner goes from an aerobic state to an anaerobic state.

GLOSSARY

Mitochondrial density – the number and quality of mitochondria in muscle cells.

Plantar flexion – pointing your foot downward, like a ballerina.

Runner's anemia – also known as iron deficiency anemia. The condition causes fatigue resulting from inadequate iron intake.

Running economy (RE) – the amount of oxygen burned at any given speed. This is a basic measure of efficiency.

Shin splints – a painful condition where the posterior tibialis muscle tears itself away from the tibia, and becomes inflamed.

Tendonitis – a condition where the tendrils of a tendon become agitated, resulting in painful inflammation.

Threshold (tempo) workouts – workouts designed to improve the speed at which a runner switches from an aerobic state to an anaerobic state. See Lactate Threshold.

VO_2 max – the maximum capacity of an individual's body to transport and use oxygen. Also called the aerobic capacity.

RESOURCES

National statistics sites

Milesplit.com

Athletic.net

Maxpreps.com

Online running magazines

Runner's World

Track & Field News

Women's Running

Trail Runner

Competitor

UltraRunning

RESOURCES

Running websites

LetsRun.com

RunRepeat.com

CoolRunning.com

Popular running books

Once a Runner, by John L. Parker Jr.

Running with the Buffaloes, by Chris Lear

Born to Run: A Hidden Tribe, Superathletes, and the Greatest Race the World Has Never Seen, by Christopher McDougall

Lore of Running, by Tim Noakes

ChiRunning, by Danny Dreyer

Dr. Nicholas Romanov's Pose Method of Running: A New Paradigm of Running, by John Robson and Nicholas Romanov

Eat and Run: My Unlikely Journey to Ultramarathon Greatness, by Scott Jurek

Running with the Kenyans: Discovering the Secrets of the Fastest People on Earth, by Adharanand Finn

My Life on the Run, by Burt Yasso

The Terrible and Wonderful Reasons Why I Run Long Distances, by Matthew Inman

Food and nutrition books

In Defense of Food: An Eater's Manifesto (Michael Pollan)

Food Rules: An Eater's Manual (Michael Pollan)

Food, Inc.

Running movies

McFarland, USA

Fire on the Track: The Steve Prefontaine Story

Without Limits

Chariots of Fire

Running Brave

Endurance

Jim Ryun: America's Greatest Miler

Prefontaine

The Jericho Mile

On the Edge

The Loneliness of the Long Distance Runner

4 Minute Mile

Saint Ralph

AFTERWORD

"Running taught me valuable lessons. In cross-country competition, training counted more than intrinsic ability, and I could compensate for a lack of natural aptitude with diligence and discipline. I applied this in everything I did."

-Nelson Mandela

Made in the USA
Monee, IL
28 October 2021